C

INTRODUCTION

INTRODUCTION

Having been a follower of Jesus for decades, I have witnessed to many acts of graciousness and self-sacrifice within the church setting. It has been encouraging to watch people of different denominations, social backgrounds, economic status, and geographical settings come together for the greater good. Being part of the life of the church for so long has allowed me to see people's lives impacted in innumerable positive ways.

However, it is no secret that the Christ's church has issues. It has been this way from the opening pages of the book of Acts. Few things cause as much frustration and disagreement within the church as does the topic of a woman's place in ministry leadership. Should women have any leadership within the church? If so, is there a limit to the level of ministry leadership a woman should be granted? These are two questions that have dominated conversations in congregations around the world.

When I first accepted an invitation to discuss this issue with a group of ministers, a friend cautioned be to "tread lightly" because emotions run hot on the topic. It didn't take long sitting on that panel to discover that what my friend had warned me about was indeed true.

The issue of a woman's leadership role in ministry is so foundational to the identity of churches that labels like "Liberal." "Prudish," and "Apostate" are terms used by some as weapons to degrade those who disagree with their personal opinions on the subject. Someone has to be correct in their assessment of a woman's role in leadership ministry. This means someone also must be misguided in their opinion. It is not an issue of conscience or preference.

To be fair to people on both sides of this volatile issue, a woman's place in ministry is foundational to the life of the church. Understanding this key issue is to understand God's role for men and women in the kingdom. Unfortunately, our emotional and cultural foundations blur the scriptural teaching on this subject to the point that many (on both sides) view it from a prism given to them by others.

In this book we will examine some key scriptures on the subject of a woman's role in leadership ministry. My focus will not be on current church practice or sociological developments which have affected people's views on the subject. Scripture will be examined as we answer the question, "Have we believed a lie?"

The first potion of the book will focus on key passages on the topic. The second portion of the book will focus on key persons within scripture.

As you read through this short book you will not find doctrinal statements, lists of church leaders agreeing with my position or national statistics showing what culture currently thinks on the topic. This will be a simple look at the scriptures themselves.

PART ONE: KEY PASSAGES

Key Passages on The Topic:

One of the most frustrating aspects of examining a topic like this is the focus on "proof text." Proof texting is the process of simply looking for verses or passages that "prove" our point while ignoring those which challenge our position. This is a dangerous practice for several reasons. First, it is just lazy. Approaching any topic and simply running through a concordance looking for verses that agree with our position isn't doing biblical study. It doesn't allow for a meaningful investigation of the Bible's meaning and message.

Second, proof texting shifts the authority on a given subject from the Bible to our interpretation of the Bible. In essence, we become the standard and force the Bible to agree with us. Few discussions are as frustrating as those where Bible verses are ripped from their original context and thrown down as "proof" of a given position.

Finally, proof texting is abusive. When we use this technique to prove our point we are actually being abusive. We are abusing the Bible itself. We are abusing people who may be hurt or disheartened by believing what we say (though the Bible doesn't actually agree with us). It is abusive to our spiritual growth because when we behave as the authority over the Bible we cannot submit ourselves to it.

In this short book we will examine the text about a woman's place in ministry within their given context.

When these context driven texts agree with our position we can take great comfort. When these context driven texts disagree with our position we will need to adjust our beliefs to align with the Bible.

Rather than focusing on every text in the entire Bible, our approach will be to deal with the major New Testament passages on the subject. Specifically, we will be dealing with the following passages:

Galatians 3:28

Luke 10:32-42

Selected texts in Acts

1 Corinthians 11:2-6

1 Corinthians 14:33-36

1 Timothy 2:8-15

Other vital passages such as Genesis 2, Genesis 3, Ephesians 5, etc., will be discussed in passing. This by no means is an attempt to suggest that these passages are of lesser value to the discussion of a women's place in public ministry. Rather, the approach is an attempt to deal with the topic in an orderly way. Enough discussion will take place on other pertinent passages, though they will be dealt with as secondary passages to shed light on their relevance.

Galatians 3:28
There is no Jew or Greek, slave or free, male or female; for you are all one in Christ Jesus.

A great injustice is done to the book of Galatians as a whole and this verse in particular when it is reduced to a "proof text" for a woman's right to take leadership roles within the church. I have lost count of the number of times this verse has been quoted and misquoted within the context of our discussion. While this is a favorite verse used on our subject it is, in fact, not dealing with a woman's place (or a man's place, for that matter) in ministry. Within the context of Galatians chapter three this verse refers to every follower of Jesus' place within the kingdom of God. Paul's emphasis in this verse, this passage, and this book is that God does not have two separate levels of acceptance within His family. Every follower of Jesus, regardless of their status in society, is an equal stakeholder in God's kingdom.

Paul's point is that Jesus' one family is made of people who all have equal standing, as the fulfillment of His promise to Abraham in Genesis 12 and Genesis 15. God's family isn't made up of members with lesser and greater access to Him. Through Jesus everyone has equal standing and responsibility before God. It is a family made up of everyone who proves his/her belief in the life, work, and death of Jesus by dedicating his/her life to following Jesus.

Most modern translations do a brilliant job of expressing Paul's use of the Greek language (Greek is the language in which Paul wrote Galatians). However, a couple modern translations haven't done as good a job as they could have in expressing Paul's words. The Greek text does not read "*neither male nor female.*" Rather, it reads "*no male or female.*" As petty as this may seem at first, it is actually quite significant. Paul is quoting Genesis chapter 1 where unity is portrayed as part of the original created order. Paul is not undoing the original created order of distinctions between male and female. Rather he is underscoring God's intent to restore, through Jesus, humanity to the place of unity found in creation. Unity doesn't mean "the same" but different creations brought into balance. This original unity also is seen in darkness and day, sky and land, water and land, etc. Consider what scripture says in Galatians 6:16, Romans 8: and 1 Corinthians 15.

The Gnostics (a religious group of Paul's day which blended Christianity and paganism into a hybrid religion) taught there was no real distinction between the sexes. Their faulty view of reality led to innumerable theological and practical problems.

Paul is quite clear that God created male and female with very real and obvious distinctions. However, these distinctions had nothing to do with one's acceptance into the family of God or one's access to Him. Hebrew society of Paul's day was extremely segregated by ethnicity, status, and gender. Because of Jesus, all these are removed and everyone has access to the One God because they are all equally part of His one family.

When we remove Galatians 3:28 from the debate over a woman's place in ministry and put the emphasis where it belongs, this verse become a source of powerful hope and peace. We do harm to both our topic - a woman's place in ministry - and the great sense of restored unity Paul intended it to be for readers if we force this verse to speak to women in ministry.

The Gospels

When reading the Gospels one of the difficulties many have in seeing a woman's place in ministry comes from perspective. It is always important to remember that the Bible was not written to us. It was written *FOR* us but not *TO* us. When we read the Bible, it is important to keep this is mind because the original recipients of the Gospels had a much different social structure than that of the modern reader. When read from a first-century perspective, the Gospels elevate the place and ministry opportunities for women in God's kingdom.

Let's begin with a quick look at the resurrection by focusing on two recorded facts. The record (written by males) show it was the male disciples who all forsook Jesus during his crucifixion. It is at this point in history, prior to Peter and the other 10 male disciples being restored, we find women coming first to Jesus' tomb. We also read that it was women who first saw and reported Jesus' physical resurrection from the dead. This is inspiring when read from a 21st century perspective. However, it becomes game changing when read from a first century perspective.

Two simultaneous facts about the early church's view of women in ministry are revealed when read from a first century perspective. First, in the first century (as today in much of the world) women were considered inferior to men in every way. This is exactly why they could freely move about as Jesus was crucified without fear of being put to death by Jewish religious leaders. Women were not considered to be a threat to the Hebrew religion or to the Roman state. They were, after all, *just women.*

Second, Jesus' kingdom viewed women differently than did the Hebrews and Romans. Women are seen by the early church as equal partners in Jesus' kingdom. This is why, in a male dominated society, the official Gospel record shows women being the first to do these things. This is actually an anti-productive historical note to place in the Gospels if the purpose was to maintain male dominant leadership. It would have been very simple to say, "followers saw and reported" rather than specifically noting *"women saw and reported."*

The reason for noting the role of women at the crucifixion and resurrection was specifically to show that in Jesus' kingdom women had equal roles to play alongside men. If women were not equal in Jesus' kingdom, their experiences and contributions would have been purposely left out or minimized.

The Luke 10:38-42 Account

While they were traveling, He entered a village, and a woman named Martha welcomed Him into her home. She had a sister named Mary, who also sat at the Lord's feet and was listening to what He said. But Martha was distracted by her many tasks, and she came up and asked, "Lord, don't You care that my sister has left me to serve alone? So tell her to give me a hand."

The Lord answered her, "Martha, Martha, you are worried and upset about many things but one thing is necessary. Mary has made the right choice, and it will not be taken away from her."

The historical account of Mary and Martha is preached and taught regularly in churches. Most often the focus is placed on how followers of Jesus should put Him first. This is an excellent and much needed message given our culture's hectic schedules. However, this truth (as important as it is) is not the main fact presented in Luke 10. The way first century readers would have viewed this text has more to do with Jesus' acceptance of women in leadership roles than with a person learning better time management.

We find Martha in a separate area of the house preparing a meal as Mary was seated at Jesus' feet. Everyone present that day, and many of readers in the Middle East today, would see this scene in an astonishingly different way than modern Western readers. That phrase *"seated at Jesus' feet"* means Mary had abandoned the women's area to sit as a disciple in the male part of the house. Mary had broken the common social convention of Jesus' day. This was scandalous enough on its own. We see Mary daring to view herself as equal to Jesus' male disciples.

However, the absolutely groundbreaking issue with this event isn't that Mary overstepped her place in the social structure. The key issue for people in the home that day and readers of Luke was that Jesus didn't send Mary back to the women's place. Other New Testament writers use this phrase to make clear that one sitting at the feet of a teacher does so to become a teacher themselves. An example of this is Paul sitting at Gamaliel's feet.

Even more dramatic than Mary overstepping social barriers and Jesus not sending her back to the woman's side was Jesus' words to Martha. Jesus said, *"Mary has chosen the good part, which will not be taken away from her."* You can almost see the shock on first-century people's faces as they read this account. Jesus Himself affirms Mary's right to sit among men as an equal disciple. This event provides a clear visual on how Jesus viewed women in ministry. Disciples sat at the feet of a teacher to become teachers themselves. Jesus completely and wholeheartedly accepted Mary's choice to become such a disciple.

The Book of Acts

It is in the book of Acts where we discover much of the meaningful insights into life as a first-century follower of Jesus. Acts is an historical/theological record of the earliest followers of Jesus. In this unique book of the Bible, we gain brilliant insight into the beliefs and practices of those closest to the death and resurrection of Jesus. Their view of women stands in vivid contrast to much of the culture around them. Because of space only the briefest of examples will be considered in this book.

Acts 1:12-14

Then they returned to Jerusalem from the mount called the Mount of Olives, which is near Jerusalem—a Sabbath day's journey away. When they arrived, they went to the room upstairs where they were staying: Peter, John, James, Andrew, Philip, Thomas, Bartholomew, Matthew, James the son of Alphaeus, Simon the Zealot, and Judas the son of James. All these were continually united in prayer, along with the women, including Mary the mother of Jesus, and His brothers. Much discussion has taken place on this passage. Questions about why only 120 people trusted the risen Jesus enough to follow these first instructions and the transformation of the disciples into men of faith are wonderful explorations. However, a significant issue is nearly missed in all the discussion, namely, the mention of women. The fact that Luke records this event as he does is far more that simple filler information. Nor was it a role call because if that were the case everyone present would have been named.

In a culture that regarded women as being a step below men, Luke's statement was impressive and of great theological importance. Listed in those who followed Jesus' first instructions in Acts are *"along with the women, including Mary the mother of Jesus."*

Luke makes a special note of females being present and by implication equal with the men listed. From the very beginning Luke's book focuses on God's restoration plan for humanity which includes raising women to their original status in Eden.

Acts 5:1-11
But a man named Ananias, with his wife Sapphira, sold a piece of property. However, he kept back part of the proceeds with his wife's knowledge, and brought a portion of it and laid it at the apostles' feet. Then Peter said, "Ananias, why has Satan filled your heart to lie to the Holy Spirit and keep back part of the proceeds from the field? Wasn't it yours while you

possessed it? And after it was sold, wasn't it at your disposal? Why is it that you planned this thing in your heart? You have not lied to men but to God!" When he heard these words, Ananias dropped dead, and a great fear came on all who heard. The young men got up, wrapped his body, carried him out, and buried him. There was an interval of about three hours; then his wife came in, not knowing what had happened. "Tell me," Peter asked her, "did you sell the field for this price?" "Yes," she said, "for that price." Then Peter said to her, "Why did you agree to test the Spirit of the Lord? Look! The feet of those who have buried your husband are at the door, and they will carry you out!" Instantly she dropped dead at his feet. When the young men came in, they found her dead, carried her out, and buried her beside her husband. Then great fear came on the whole church and on all who heard these things.

Much of twenty-first century church life has been built upon the idea that a woman's place is subjugated to her man. The event recorded here by Luke reveals God's view of husbands and wives in His kingdom is far different. Had God viewed women the way modern Christianity does, this woman would have been spared. After all, the wife would simply have been following the leadership of her husband. She should have been rewarded as a faithful wife who submitted to her husband. Why would a just God punish this woman for faithfully submitting the husband God gave her? It is impossible to join the justice of God, the death of this wife, and a woman's subjugation to her man. The only way to rectify these problems in this text is by viewing it as the first-century did.

The way those present that day viewed these events reveals the equality of men and women in God's kingdom. The reason this wife was punished for her part in the deception is precisely because she was equally involved. Rather than blindly following her husband's instructions they evidently approached their marriage as equal participants. Her thoughts, comments, and commitment to this deception were viewed by God as equally valued with that of her husband.

Acts 8:1-3
Saul agreed with putting him to death. On that day a severe persecution broke out against the church in Jerusalem, and all except the apostles were scattered throughout the land of Judea and Samaria. Devout men buried Stephen and mourned deeply over him. Saul, however, was ravaging the church. He would enter house after house, drag off men and women, and put them in prison.

For our purposes the key line of what Luke records in the last one – *"He would enter house after house, drag off men and women, and put them in prison.*" It is highly significant that Luke records Saul's treatment of Christian men and women as equals. First-century Hebrews viewed women as having lesser value and, by default, a non-threat. However, Luke reports that the Church's view of women was one of equals and therefore an equal threat to the established Jewish religion. Precisely because of this view of a woman's equality to a man, Saul was given authority to treat Christian women equally with Christian men. The thought of ministry equality within the first century church is unsettling to some in the twenty-first century. However, the fact still remains that women in first century Christianity were living in the same ministry capacity as their male counterparts.

Acts 21:7-9

When we completed our voyage from Tyre, we reached Ptolemais, where we greeted the brothers and stayed with them one day. The next day we left and came to Caesarea, where we entered the house of Philip the evangelist, who was one of the Seven, and stayed with him. This man had four virgin daughters who prophesied.

Tucked away in this great section of Acts 21 is an amazing line in verse nine, "*This man had four virgin daughters who prophesied.*" This line has zero impact on the flow of events in chapter 21. Reading this line, we have only two real options for consideration. First, Luke is giving a simple recognition to Philip by graciously providing recognition to his daughters. Given Luke's focus in Acts this is unlikely.

Second, and more in keeping with the structure of Acts itself, Luke is giving us an historical/theological view of God's kingdom. It is true that the addition of this line in verse nine doesn't affect the flow of events in chapter twenty-one. However, it is equally true that Luke records this line to show God was equally using women and men in all aspects of ministry including prophecy. What is often viewed as mere background information on Philip's family is, in reality, a bold statement by Luke about a women's place in the ministry life of the Church.

THE EPISTLES

As a matter of record, I believe it is vital to note how the Epistles should be read. It sounds a bit silly but, in reality, it is a profound truth that helps unlock the true message of the Epistles. The key to understanding the Epistles is to read them in light of the Gospels/Acts. Often we read the New Testament in reverse. We do this by examining Jesus' words and actions (along with the words and actions of the church in Acts) through the lens of what the Epistles say. This approach is completely reversed from how the New Testament should be understood.

It is important to keep in mind that the Epistles were written to explain and expand upon the Gospels/Acts rather than the other way around. This approach not only is more faithful to the text itself but also opens much of the Epistle's message up more fully. With this principle in mind we keep what the Gospels/Acts have said while we walk through these examples in the Epistles.

1 Corinthians 11:2-16
Now I praise you because you always remember me and keep the traditions just as I delivered them to you. But I want you to know that Christ is the head of every man, and the man is the head of the woman, and God is the head of Christ. Every man who prays or prophesies with something on his

head dishonors his head. But every woman who prays or prophesies with her head uncovered dishonors her head, since that is one and the same as having her head shaved. So if a woman's head is not covered, her hair should be cut off. But if it is disgraceful for a woman to have her hair cut off or her head shaved, she should be covered. A man, in fact, should not cover his head, because he is God's image and glory, but woman is man's glory. For man did not come from woman, but woman came from man. And man was not created for woman, but woman for man. This is why a woman should have a symbol of authority on her head, because of the angels. In the Lord, however, woman is not independent of man, and man is not independent of woman. For just as woman came from man, so man comes through woman, and all things come from God. Judge for yourselves: Is it proper for a woman to pray to God with her head uncovered? Does not even nature itself teach you that if a man has long hair it is a disgrace to him, but that if a woman has long hair, it is her glory? For her hair is given to her as a covering. But if anyone wants to argue about this, we have no other custom, nor do the churches of God.

One must work with great vigor to make this text imply Paul that is teaching women should not take part in public church services. Make no mistake; There are those who believe they are up to the task. Their position on the subject disallows for Paul's meaning to be honestly considered. An honest reading of this passage shows Paul's instruction about *HOW* women and men are to distinguish themselves *WHILE* they lead public services. To say anything else is to blindly and willfully ignore what the text honestly teaches.

Paul's point in this passage is to show how men and women are to worship God in a way that also celebrates their gender. Understanding this demands that we know a bit about the sociological context in which it was first read. Corinthians marked gender mainly through hair and clothing styles. Art and literature of the period reveal women had long, braided hair which they covered with a scarf. The way in which a woman would distinguish herself as a prostitute in Corinth was by being in public without wearing a scarf covering their hair.

It is highly probable that some women in the Corinth church had taken Paul's words in Galatians 3:28 too far in church worship. Women were leading in the church without wearing their culturally mandated head coverings. Remember, this was a sign of prostitution. The head covering was a sociological symbol of a woman's faithfulness to her father or to her husband. As these women were taking their freedom in Christ farther than God designed, they were unwittingly saying to the culture that they had no obligation to their father or, if married, to their husband.

Paul's emphasis here is on how men and women are to look as they lead and worship at church. What Paul is not doing in this text is undoing everything the Gospels and Acts teach on women and men in the kingdom. Paul is insisting that men should lead as men and women should lead as women without blurring the clearly defined lines of human sexuality. God is honored when men lead in the church without compromising their masculinity. God is equally honored when women lead in the church without compromising their femininity. Leading without blurring the lines of human sexually stood in stark contrast to the way pagans in the Corinth community worshipped and lead. This issue isn't subjugation of women to the nursery or church kitchen but the subjugation of both sexes to leading while honoring God as male and female.

1 Corinthians 14:33-36
As in all the churches of the saints, the women should be silent in the churches, for they are not permitted to speak, but should be submissive, as the law also says. And if they want to learn something, they should ask their own husbands at home, for it is disgraceful for a woman to speak in the church meeting. Did the word of God originate from you, or did it come to you only?

I often joke that if I had a dollar for every time someone quoted this passage in a discussion on the topic of a woman's place in ministry, I could buy a yacht. On a few occasions someone has been so locked onto this passage, I've wondered if it was the only text in the Bible they knew by heart. On the flip side are those who try to ignore this passage or say it simply no longer applies. Both approaches reveal a personal bias on the topic and are unacceptable for those wanting to honor God with their examination of Scripture.

It is worth noting that when this was written, just as it is today in much of Lebanon, Syria, and Egypt, Christians worshiped in formal Arabic. This was a language which most men but only a minute number of women would know. It is also interesting that today in those parts of the world, as it was when Paul penned these instructions, the church service was physically divided with women on one side and men on the other side.

You can imagine without much difficulty the problems such circumstances would produce. A group of people (women) in a setting where most of what takes place is in a foreign language while sitting among friends.

Imagine yourself in such a setting - disconnected from what is being taught because of language barriers and sitting next to your friends. As these women (not because they were women but because they were disconnected from what was being taught and they were sitting with friends) would begin to quietly talk among themselves. As is almost always the case, quiet talking would grow louder and louder as time passed. Someone would tell the talkers to be quiet and they would. However, the cycle would continue to repeat itself again and again.

It is impressive that Paul's solution to the cultural issue wasn't to singlehandedly begin a reform moment in Corinth. He didn't demand that families sit together in church. Nor did he demand that they conduct the whole service in the common language of Greek. Much progress was already being made as 1 Corinthians 11:2-9 points out. A great deal of freedom was given to each church, so it could develop along a sociological framework which best fit the culture it was reaching. Paul's instruction was designed to minimize the immediate disruption and allow the church to develop on its own terms. This included the statements we read in this passage:

1 Timothy 2:8-15
Therefore I want the men in every place to pray, lifting up holy hands without anger or argument. Also, the women are to dress themselves in modest clothing, with decency and good sense; not with elaborate hairstyles, gold, pearls, or expensive apparel, but with good works, as is proper for women who affirm that they worship God. A woman should learn in silence with full submission. I do not allow a woman to teach or to have authority over a man; instead, she is to be silent. For Adam was created first, then Eve. And Adam was not deceived,

but the woman was deceived and transgressed. But she will be saved through childbearing, if she continues in faith, love, and holiness, with good sense.

In what now seems to be a million years ago as a first semester Bible college student I heard a professor say something which has been a guide for me all these years. While I do not recall the professor's name I do recall his statement, *"Context clears up confusion."* This powerful four-word sentence has become a foundation upon which I have studied scripture for years. One of the places it applies is certainly this passage.

The sociological context for Paul's words to Timothy and the church was first-century Ephesus which was the home to the great Greek Temple of Artemis (Romans called it the Temple of Diana). This temple was a massive building which dominated the Ephesian landscape. All of its priests were women. Because the first century Roman world (and Jewish for that matter) had no separation between religious and secular life, it meant that women dominated public life as well as religious life. The easiest way to understand this situation it is to view it as the exact opposite from Jewish culture where men dominated the religious and social life.

It isn't difficult to imagine the task Timothy had attempting to lead congregations in a culture that subjugated men in the way other cultures subjugated women. Paul's teaching to Timothy and, by default, to the Ephesian churches emphasized worship which distinguished them from the pagan worship of Artemis. It is designed as both a prohibition and a protection for the church. It acts as a prohibition, so outsiders would not confuse Christianity as an offshoot of Artemis' false religion. It functions as a protection for women against overzealous men who wished to subjugate them to a place of being lesser than men. Note the statement "*A woman should learn*" is designed to build up rather than to tear down.

Given this sociological context Paul's words clear up the confusion we in the twenty-first century have caused. With this background let's take a look at the text itself. Verse eight tells men to devote themselves to prayer rather than to following the cultural example of Ephesian society. The key to unlocking Paul's meaning is the word "*also*" in verse nine. The placement of the word "*also*" between the instructions to men and the instructions to women shows that the teaching applies to both sexes. What is extraordinary for the purposes of our topic in this book is that verses nine and ten make the same point about women. In three simple verses Paul places men and women in a position of equal footing with God regarding ministry.

All the information Paul gives us on the topic is tossed to the side by some when we get to the section stating, *"A woman should learn in silence with full submission. I do not allow a woman to teach or to have authority over a man; instead, she is to be silent."* Somehow this statement becomes the banner call for those refusing to allow women a place of leadership within the Church.

Once we remove our cultural bias from the text a whole new perspective reveals itself. It is a perspective which aligns itself with the Gospels and Acts. Remember that the Epistles are to be read in light of the Gospels/Acts. Using the Gospels/Acts as a foundation from which this passage is viewed we discover a more fitting understanding of the phrase *"with full submission"* and *"I do not allow a woman to teach or to have authority over a man; instead, she*

is to be silent." Given the culture the
Ephesian church found itself in and the
teachings of the Gospels/Acts it seems
fair to say Paul was saying, "*Women are
not the new authority within the church
over men like the Artemis cult/culture
teaches.*" It is worth noting that such a
statement is often dismissed outright by
some. However, it does fit the cultural
context and the foundation of the
Gospels and Acts perfectly.

Remember that Paul is writing to a new
movement (Christianity) based in a
female dominated culture. He needed to
emphasis the equality of the sexes
before God without over stressing one
above the other. He was encouraging
them to organize their churches with
God's view of unity being reflected in
creation (Genesis 1 and 2). His
reference to creation doesn't imply
(within the context) men are to dominate
women in church. Rather, the exact
opposite is implied, namely, that women
are not to dominate men in church. It is

the same message of unity Jesus spoke about in the Gospels and the church implemented in the book of Acts.

A beneficial way to translate Paul's words in verses eleven through fifteen from the Greek might be:
"They must be allowed to study without hassle, in full submission to God. I'm not commanding that women should teach men or try to dominate them; they should be left undisturbed. Adam was created first, you see, and then Eve; and Adam was not deceived, but the woman was deceived, and fell into sin. She will, however, be kept safe through the process of childbirth, as she continues in faith, love and holiness with prudence."

Now that we have briefly examined just a few key passages in the New Testament on our topic, we will move to the second half of the book and look specifically at key female leaders within the church.

PART 2: KEY PERSONS

Key Persons in Scripture:

The early Church, like that of the twenty-first century, was a living organism. In the first century, like today, the Church was forced to make adjustments, to clarify positions, and to live within a culture that was hostile to its existence and message. Every reader of the New Testament does themselves a genuine disservice when they fail to consider the fact that those within its pages were actual people. These people were individuals coming for various backgrounds, carrying a variety of baggage from their pasts. The New Testament does provide us with God's interaction with people. However, it also provides us with a glimpse of the interaction of people with others. Reading the New Testament with this in mind opens its pages up to a multidimensional understanding.

In this section we will briefly examine some of the key women who held leadership positions within the first-century church. There are those who hold that the ladies listed in the New Testament didn't hold leadership positions. Their assertion is that those who see New Testament women in leadership when they read the Bible do so because they want to see it. In other words, they claim those seeing women in leadership positions are reading into the text what they wish to see. It is worth noting that the reverse is also true. Those who don't see New Testament women in leadership positions fail to see it because they are looking for their absence.

What follows is biblical information regarding specific women. As with all issues, we do well to examine what is there and what is absent from the text with an attitude willing to adjust to the information gained by reading. The key figures receiving attention in this portion of the book will include the following:

Mary

Martha

Junia

Philip's four daughters

Priscilla

Eudia

Syntyche

Phoebe

Nympha

Chloe

Stephanas (also translated Stephana)

Junia in Romans 16:7
Greet Andronicus and Junia, my fellow countrymen and fellow prisoners. They are outstanding among the apostles, and were also in Christ before me.

Romans chapter 16 is one of those sections of scripture which many rush through because of the long lists of names. To do so causes one to miss a major theme of the book of Romans which is the unity Jesus provides. In this verse Paul greets Junia, a Roman woman who converted to Christ prior to Paul's visit. The phrase at issue for us are the four words *"outstanding among the apostles."* This is a great statement even if it had referred to a male because it shows the growing number of people considered to be apostles by the early church.

The phrase becomes more important when we understand that Junia was a common female name and that there are no historical examples of any male being named Junia. Unless this is the only recorded male in the entire Roman Empire with the female name "Junia," Paul was commending a female as being outstanding among the apostles. Andronicus is believed to be Junia's husband which fits the common pattern of greeting for couples.

One of the ways people deal with this woman being praised in this manner is to retranslate the word *"among."* They change the word to read *"by"* the apostles. This change is significant because it downgrades Junia's status from being an outstanding apostle to a woman *"who is thought well of"* by the apostles. The difficulty with this retranslation is that it is not faithful to the text. Regardless of what a person chooses to make of this phrase, one should not change the words to fit an opinion.

Philip's four daughters in Acts 21:8, 9
The next day we left and came to Caesarea, where we entered the house of Philip the evangelist, who was one of the Seven, and stayed with him. This man had four virgin daughters who prophesied.

In a similar way as Junia's mention in the New Testament, we are only given the most basic information about these four women. In the face of limited information, the facts we do have become more valuable. Here is what we are told about these four females:

>They were women.
>They were virgins.
>They were daughters of Philip (one of the first seven deacons and also an evangelist).
>They prophesied.

Here is it important to note that none of these four items proves, or even hints at, them being pastors, evangelists, apostles

or prophets within the church.
However, it does show with great clarity
that these four ladies did prophesy.
Because prophecy is a verbal
expression, these four ladies ministered
through prophesy in the exact way their
male counterparts did.

Priscilla in Acts 18:24-26

*A Jew named Apollos, a native
Alexandrian, an eloquent man who
was powerful in the Scriptures, arrived
in Ephesus. This man had been
instructed in the way of the Lord; and
being fervent in spirit, he spoke and
taught the things about Jesus
accurately, although he knew only of
John's baptism. After Priscilla and
Aquila heard him, they took him home
and explained the way of God to him
more accurately.*

Priscilla and Aquila pop up more than
once in the New Testament. They were
a ministry couple who worked closely

with Paul as seen in Acts 18:18-22 and Romans 16:3-5. We gain some key insights to consider about how Jesus uses men and women in ministry through the brief bits of information given about Priscilla and Aquila. First, is the obvious fact that they were a couple in ministry. In the passages which mention this couple, we don't get the sense that Priscilla is viewed as a silent partner in ministry or the one who watched the kids while Aquila taught. They are very much portrayed as partners in ministry together.

Second, (as seen in our present passage) Pricilla is actively involved in teaching a male – *"they took him home and explained the way of God to him more accurately."* In addition to the fact that she was teaching a man is that she was teaching a male teacher – Apollos. Third, because of the way this couple is always introduced in scripture it seems quite clear (though this is conjecture) that the woman took the leading role of public ministry for this couple. To be fair let me restate that this is conjecture based upon the way they are introduced. However, it is most certainly a safe conjecture. Rather than using the common introduction of male (Aquila) and his wife (Priscilla) prominence is always given to the wife Priscilla and Aquila. This is true of this couple each time they are mentioned in Scripture.

Eudia and Syntyche in Philippians 4:2, 3

I urge Eudia and I urge Syntyche to agree in the Lord. Yes, I also ask you, true partner, to help these women who have contended for the gospel at my side, along with Clement and the rest of my co-workers whose names are in the book of life.

Admittedly, I've always enjoyed listening to Pastors wrestle with this passage in sermons. Inevitably, someone preaching through this passage find himself/herself walking carefully when there are those in the congregation to whom it applies. Here we see that there are two women who contended for the gospel with Paul and other male leaders.

Paul's wording here helps clear up their public leadership role in Philippi. *Contended* is from the Greek word *sunathleo* (pronounced "soon-ath-leh'-o). It means *"to wrestle in company with."* This provides an important insight into the public role of these women within church life. These two women had publicly wrestled with words (for we know Paul's teaching against public violence when contending for the kingdom because of statements such as Ephesians 6:12) alongside Paul and other male leaders. The leadership roles of these ladies served to compound the problems of their disagreement. In other words, their leadership roles made their need to resolve the conflict of greater importance than had they simply been congregants.

Phoebe in Romans 16:1, 2

I commend to you our sister Phoebe, who is a servant of the church in Cenchreae. So you should welcome her in the Lord in a manner worthy of the saints, and assist her in whatever matter she may require you help. For indeed she has been a benefactor of many and of me also.

Here we discover a woman being introduced as *"a servant of the church in Cenchrea."* The Greek word translated *"servant"* here is also translated *"minister"* in 22 other New Testament passages including Matthew 20:26; Mark 10:43; Romans 13:4,8; 2 Corinthians 3:6; 2 Corinthians 6:4; 2 Corinthians 11:15, 23; Galatians 2:17; Ephesians 3:7; Ephesians 6:21; Colossians 1:7, 23, 25; and 1 Timothy 4:6.

Phoebe, a woman, is thought to have been the very person entrusted with bringing this letter of Romans to the church at Roman. This was no small task considering it was a trip of approximately 800 miles.

Phoebe was also described as a *"benefactor."* Other Bible translations use the word *"helper."* Both of these translations of the original Greek word are accurate. However, because of our distance from the writing of this letter to the Romans, it is helpful to look at the word Paul chose more closely.

Benefactor is translated from the Greek word *"prostatis"* and carried the meaning of *"a woman set over others, a female guardian, caring for the affairs of others and aiding them with her resources."* This is vitally important because Phoebe wasn't a servant girl who also happened to be part of the church in Cenchreae. Rather, she was a woman who served over others in the church at Cenchreae.

Nympha in Colossians 4:15

Give my greetings to the brothers in Laodicea, and to Nympha and the church in her house.

Nympha was a woman mentioned among the other leaders in churches (Colossians 4:7-18). She is greeted along with the *"church in her house."* Due to the absence of a husband or father attached to this greeting, we can surmise one of two things. First, we can surmise that she was single and wealthy enough to own her home or that her unsaved father/husband allowed the church to meet in the home.

Second, regardless of which of the above statements be true, one cannot deny that she was in charge of the house church. Most likely she would have been the Pastor of the church which met in her house. There is no textual or historic evidence to the contrary.

Lydia in Acts 16:14, 15
A woman named Lydia, a dealer in purple cloth from the city of Thyatira, who worshiped God, was listening. The Lord opened her heart to pay attention to what was spoken by Paul. After she and her household were baptized, she urged us, "If you consider me a believer in the Lord, come and stay at my house." And she persuaded us.

Lydia is seen as supporting the ministry by opening her home as a church. It is important to note that this continued even as Paul and Timothy were jailed – Acts 16:40. This is significant because with Paul and Timothy in jail they were unable to physically lead the services. It is also worth noting that many claim Lydia was only a woman who opened her home for the church to use and that she most likely got permission from her husband to do so. However, (as with Nymphia in Colossians 4:15) there is no information given which leads to such a conclusion.

Chloe in 1 Corinthians 1:11
For it has been reported to me about you, my brothers, by members of Chloe's household, that there are quarrels among you.

The word translated as *"household"* here is also translated *"people"* in various other New Testament texts. There is simply no way of knowing for certain if Paul is referring here to people who are related to a female follower of Jesus or to people who are part of her house church.

The purpose for making note of this passages, with all its ambiguity on the subject, is to point out that here (as in other places) Paul refers to a female rather than to a male as the head of a given group. This alone reveals the early Church's stance on men and women being equal before God in all aspects of life and responsibility.

Stephanas (also translated Stephana) in 1 Corinthians 16:15-16
Brothers, you know the household of Stephanas: they are the firstfruits of Achaia and have devoted themselves to serving the saints. I urge you also to submit to such people, and to everyone who works and labors with them.

Stephanas is the female form of the name Stephen. Stephanas and her household were Paul's first converts in Achaia. Please note two key textual issues here. First, some translations substitutes *"submit to such people"* (an accurate translation) with *"submit to such men"* (an inaccurate translation). Making this change from people to men leaves the reader with the impression that Paul is telling the Corinthians to submit themselves to the authority of the men of Stephanas' household but she is excluded from receiving such respect as a church leader.

Second, Paul seems to be correcting the Corinthians for not giving Stephanas and those working with her respect as leaders. This being the case, the twenty-first century Church may do well to consider its treatment of women in ministry positions.

Third, because the larger passage clearly speaks of church ministers, it would be a violation to the flow of this text to somehow conclude that simply because Stephanas is a woman that she is excluded from being a leader in the church. In fact, the opposite is true – Stephanas' ministry as a minister/leader is strengthened by the fact that Paul discusses her in a section dealing with ministers/leaders.

Even a brief discussion of key women in ministry positions like these here shows the first-century church living out the teachings of the Jesus.

CONCLUDING REMARKS

Concluding Remarks

Dealing with a volatile issue like women in ministry is extraordinarily emotional. Each of us brings to the discussion our biases, personal examples, and preferences. Each of these will color our perspective as we read the biblical text. To say otherwise reflects our lack of self-awareness. Yet, if we are to become mature individual followers of Jesus and a Church which reflects an honest depiction of the kingdom of God, we must choose to deal with the text.

Recently I was in a discussion group for local ministers from various denominations. Our topic that day was precisely the issue this book addresses. The conversation and comments grew increasingly sharp as leaders from various perspectives attempted to show the biblical reasons for their perspectives on a woman's place in ministry. To everyone's credit the conversion stayed on topic (mostly) and no one stormed out of the meeting.
After the discussion group adjourned and we made our way to the parking lot, a

friend of mine who is a wonderful minister jokingly said to me, *"I don't care what anyone says God knows I'm right."* What my minister friend said in jest I fear many hold as a truth. They view their opinion on the topic as correct and that God is on their side. We would all do well to examine and then reexamine our most closely held views.

It is this type of humble examination of scripture that allows each of us to more fully embrace the truths of the Bible. It is also this same humility that allows us to discard or adjust erroneous views of scripture. Without humility and a willingness to correct errors in our beliefs, we continue to perpetuate false views God and the Church.

It is a sign of great arrogance to approach the Bible with the underlying attitude of making passages fit our preexisting opinions. Both views – a woman is equally valued by God as a leader and a woman is subservient to a man as a leader – cannot be correct. Each of us would do well to approach this topic in humility allowing the text to shape our view.

Regardless of the conclusion you have come to after reading this book, it is my hope that it offered an opportunity to reexamine the topic.